# Between the Mountain and the Land Lies the Lesson

## Poetic Midrash on Sacred Community
### Bamidbar through Devarim

I0175043

*Abe Mezrich*

**Ben Yehuda Press**
Teaneck, New Jersey

Published by Ben Yehuda Press
122 Ayers Court #1B
Teaneck, NJ  07666

http://www.BenYehudaPress.com

To subscribe to our monthly book club and support independent Jewish publishing, visit https://www.patreon.com/BenYehudaPress

**Jewish Poetry Project #14**                               **http://jpoetry.us**

Ben Yehuda Press books may be purchased at a discount by synagogues, book clubs, and other institutions buying in bulk. For information, please email markets@BenYehudaPress.com

ISBN13 978-1-934730-82-9

19 20 21/ 10 9 8 7 6 5 4 3 2 1        20200428

# Contents

# Between the Mountain and the Land is the Lesson

*Poetic Midrash on Sacred Community*

*Abe Mezrich*

# Notes on Translation, Transliteration, and the Names of God

1. *The translations throughout this book are mostly my own, with help from the Jewish Publication Society (JPS) Tanakh when I wasn't sure how best to render a word or phrase into English.*

2. *I have not always been consistent with how I transliterate Hebrew words, and how I refer to the various names of God, from poem to poem.*

3. *There are many ways to express the truth.*

*–AM*

*Abe Mezrich*

# Where We Begin

The Torah is five books. But it is also a story in three acts.
Act One is creation: of the universe, of one family, of a people.
That first act takes us from the Genesis of time through the
Exodus of a slave nation into peoplehood.

Act Two is the heart of the Torah: our time at the Mountain.
We encounter God. We are given His Law. We make a home
for Him through the Mishkan.

Then, finally, Act Three. Moses sends spies from the Mountain
over to the Land.

The journey starts again. This time, it is the journey of a com-
munity of God.

But what will a community of God be like? In the journey we
find the beginnings of an answer.

*Abe Mezrich*

# The Journey
## Shelach Licha
## through Ma'Asei

*You have spent too much time at the Mountain,* God tells Moses at the opening of *Bamidbar—The Book of Numbers.*

*Go forth.*

And for the first three *parshiot* of the BaMidbar, the people mobilize to do just that.

In the fourth parsha, *Shelach Licha,* the first of the people—the spies—set foot in the Land. They have gone forth.

Let us go forth too.

·

*Abe Mezrich*

# Shelach Licha

# Asking

1.
The people see the giant fruit of the Land
& hear of the giants of the Land
& draw their conclusions
& become hysterical.
For this, they never enter the Land.

But later a man gathers wood on Sabbath
and the people do not know what to do
and inquire of God.
God answers.

2.
The upright do not draw their own conclusions.
They know they do not know the answer
and turn, instead, to the question.
Answers are God's work.

*Numbers 13:1 – 14:3; 15:32-36*

*Abe Mezrich*

# Setting Out

Aaron's sons offer a strange fire & are consumed.
        God invites Aaron into the Holy of Holies.

Israel tries to take the Land without God's permission.
Without God's help, the people are beaten back.
        Then God teaches the Laws to keep in the Land.

We break the rules and begin the journey.
Sometimes, God shows us the rest of the way.

*Leviticus 10:1-2; Leviticus Chapter 16; Numbers 14:40-15:31*

## Land of Vows

The spies come back and say: That Land is dangerous.
Mob panic ensues. The people refuse to move ahead.

The first Law that God teaches next
is a Law of Vows.
When you come to the Land, God says,
and vow an offering,
this is what you must do.

A vow is what you have taken upon yourself.
It has nothing to do with the people around you.
It is an embodiment of your own personal steadfastness.
A vow is the opposite of mob panic.

We come to the Land as a people
but only they who come to the Land and vow
    who can shut out the shouts against truth
    and take their own offering up to God—
only they will enter.


*Numbers 13:1 – 14:3; 15:1-3*

*Abe Mezrich*

# When Life Frightens You

1.
God tells Moses:
send spies into the Land.
Moses tells them:
*Be strong*
be brave
take from the Land's fruits.
This, in the time
of the year's first grapes.

When the spies report back
holding up the Land's fruit,
fear overtakes them.
They sow panic.
They are not strong
or brave:
they forget
that God is their strength.


2.
Later, God says:
In the Land,
on your farms,
take from the first fruits of your field,
bring that fruit to the Temple,
declare how God has taken you
from Egypt
to this Land,
to your crop.

Recognizing God's Hand like this,
each farmer reverses the work of the spies
who feared to truly possess
the first fruits they held.

3.
Of course this equates the spies
terrified at a strange new place
with a farmer tending his own soil
every year.

\*

There is the fear of what is new
and there is the fear of the life you know.
In either fear,
all is possible
with God's help.

*Numbers 13:1 – 14:3; Deuteronomy 26:1-11*

*Abe Mezrich*

# Korach

## Incensed

Korach says: We are all holy & should serve before God.
Yet when Korach's followers offer incense
at the front of the holy Tent of Meeting—
God punishes them.

Later, Moses sends Aaron to burn incense right in the
midst of the people.

Perhaps Moses knows:
"We are holy" does not mean
we should charge into holy space.

It means we are holy space.


*Numbers Chapter 16, 17:9-15*


　　　　　　　*Abe Mezrich*

# Why Ideals Are Unclear

1.
Korach leads a rebellion against Moses
and against Aaron.
God tells Moses and Aaron:
Separate from these rebels
and I will devour them.
But Moses and Aaron pray
that God have mercy.
*

And when rebellion fans out
across the nation
God sends His plague.
Moses tells Aaron:
take incense,
stand between the dead
and the living;
and where Aaron stands
the plague stops.

2.
God made the world
separating Light from Darkness,
dividing the universe
along clear lines of Truth.
Now, God will separate
Moses and Aaron
from the rebels,
from the wicked ones.

3.
But Moses and Aaron
will not be separated out
and Moses sends Aaron
to stand amidst the sinners.

God rules the world
through the clear divisions of Truth
but Moses and Aaron lead
as heads of a nation
as leaders of a people
good and wicked.

4.
We are led by God.
We are led, also, by Moses,
whom God has chosen to lead us.
Led by God
led by Moses
we are defined by their conversation
between Divine Truth,
human truth.

*Genesis Chapter 1; Numbers 16:20-21, 17:9-15*

# After, Law

1.
After Korach rebels
and after the people rebel
and after God punishes
and after God proves
and after the people, finally, fear—
then God commands Law.


2.
Law is a kind of promise.

Offering Law, God says:
We will be together for a very long time.
Offering Law, God says:
you are capable of a holy life.

If God did not think this,
handing out rules would make no sense.


3.
Sometimes there is rebellion
or the ground opens up from below
but the fabric of our closeness does not change.

That is the promise of Law.


*Based on the thinking of Rav Soloveitchik as described by Pinchas Peli*
*Numbers Chapters 16 - 19*

# Why Aaron

All along
God punishes the rebels against Aaron's priesthood.
But God does not openly prove Aaron's priesthood
through a miracle
        (a dry stick growing flowers)
until Aaron stands in the middle of the people
holding the incense
to block the plague
by which God punishes the rebellion.

Then, Aaron is a priest against God
and a priest against himself
and a priest on behalf of the people.
And God chooses him.


*Numbers 17:9-27*

# Chukat

## This is Good Government

Korach asks Moses:
Why do you and Aaron lord yourselves over Israel?
We are all holy.

Korach leads a rebellion based on this question.
God punishes Korach's whole following bitterly for this.

But later Israel rallies to save a prisoner captured in war.
The entire nation, the Torah says, rallies together.
The whole people; but Moses is not mentioned anywhere.

Here is Korach's idea of mass leadership.
Except it is not about power.
It is about caring for each other.

*Numbers 16:1-3, 21:1-3, 32-34*

# What Can We Offer Mourners?

1.
God tells Moses:
Take *a pure, red cow*
*that has never borne a yoke.*
Slaughter it,
burn it to ash,
set the ash in water.
When a man touches a corpse
or a grave,
the priest should sprinkle the man with the ash-water,
making him pure again.

2.
This ceremony is unlike sacrifices
—another duty of the priests—
which are *pleasing aromas to God,*
smoke rising upward.
Here is a ceremony of ash,
char on the earth.
*
And what of the color red?
The color of blood,
that holds the soul—
life coursing in the body;
the color of the hair
of Esau the hunter,
the man of strength.
*
Cattle are creatures of strength,
meant to bear the yoke.
A cow yet to bear the yoke
is strength-in-waiting.
Cows,
mothers of cattle,

are strength-in-waiting.
*

So this is a ceremony of the strength of life.
That is the ceremony we bring to death.


3.
A man who encounters death
could become consumed by it.
We touch him with this ash-water,
we tell him: come back to this world,
to the strength of the living earth,
to the strength of this red cow.


*Genesis 25:25; Leviticus Chapter 1, 17:11; Numbers Chapter 19*

*Abe Mezrich*

# View the Snake

1.
The wily Snake tricks the Woman
into trading Eden for fruit.

The Woman tells the Man about this fruit
and the Man eats also.

God confronts them,
the Man says *The Woman whom you have given me
told me to eat.*

2.
The Snake will not commit his own sin.
The Man will not own to having committed sin.
No one will admit to having given a world away
on account of a fruit.

3.
God proclaims
that snakes shall strike humankind at the heel
and that we humans will strike the snakes from up above.

A war of never looking the enemy in the eye,
never staring your guilt in the face.

4.
Jacob,
who is also wily,
whose name *Yaakov*
recalls how he was born
clutching Esau's *eikev,* his *heel,*
from behind,
talks Esau into trading his birthright for stew
tricks his blind father into giving over Esau's blessing

for a meal
and never (that we see)
says a word of it to either of them, after.
Our ancestor has something in common with the Snake.


5.
The people Israel,
Jacob's children,
pass Edom
—the land of Esau's children—
but do not enter Edom's land.

And the people crave food there
and curse God's manna
and God sends poisonous snakes.

We have sinned before God and before you,
they tell Moses
which is to say
that they apologize wholly.

And God tells them:
Make a statue of a serpent;
whoever has been bitten by a snake
will look up at the statue and live.

6.
With no Edom there, no Esau,
they have no one to trick into wrongdoing
and no one to hand their blame to.

They are ready to learn:
They can raise their heads
they can take the next step
they can look the snake in the eye.


*Genesis 3, 25:26, 29-34, 27; Numbers 21:4-9*

*Abe Mezrich*

# Staff / Snake

1.
The people *speak against God,*
and God sends poisonous snakes to punish them.

Then the people repent.

*We have sinned,* they say.

God instructs Moses to erect a pole,
and on it to place a serpent of brass.

Anyone who is bitten by a snake
will look at this pole with this snake,
and will live.

2.
A pole is a symbol of a person or a people.
Consider a flagstaff, or a scepter.

A snake is really an animated stick. It is a pole come to life,

as when Aaron cast his staff before Pharaoh
at the command of God
and the staff became a serpent, hissing at Pharaoh's feet

as if to say: Our staff,
our symbol,
has come to life to strike you.

3.
Now, the people Israel encounter snakes.

And they look at their own deed and repent.
Which is to say: they seek out the meaning behind things,
the staff from which these snakes come.

They unite the world of symbol with the world of life.

They marry the snake and the pole
and in this marriage,
healing comes.


*Exodus 7:8-12; Numbers 21:4-9*


*Abe Mezrich*

# Balak

# Who can speak?

1.
The prophet Bilam's donkey sees the angel of God.
Frightened animal,
she crouches to keep distance.
Then God *opened the donkey's mouth*
and the donkey speaks.
Then Bilam, too, sees the angel.

2.
It is someone unquestioning in her vision
a scared animal
with a strong back
who knows only how to carry a load
and how to act on what she sees—
who can do such precise work,
such lifting,
as to carry a holy vision to the world.

It is she
who can truly speak.


*Numbers 22:27-31*

*Abe Mezrich*

# Religion Without Community

1.
The prophet Bila'am leaves *the land of the children of his
people.*

Far from his people,
he may utter only the words of prophecy
that *God* has *put in* his *mouth.*

2.
But even so Bila'am *saw Israel dwelling tribe by tribe*
and just then *the spirit of God was upon him*

and Bila'am says
in his own words:
*How good are your tents, o Jacob; your dwellings, o Israel.*

3.
You can mouth God's truth anywhere.
But only looking to the tribe
can your own words become God's.


*Numbers 22:28; 24:2-5*

# Where to Look

Before our journey ends we find new ways of seeing ourselves, the nations, God. The vantage points of the enemy king, the foreign prophet, the mystic animal; of the overlook where you see our tents from afar; of nations and their fates at the end of days.

We cannot arrive until we learn to see as the world sees.

*Numbers Chapter 22- 24*

# Looking, Seeing / Cursing, Blessing

1.

King Balak shows the prophet Bilam a view of Israel
from angle after angle, overlook after overlook,
hoping this vision will send God's curse
flying from Bilam's mouth.

2.

Finally Bilam sees *it is good in HaShem's eyes*
*to bless Israel* and not to curse it;

and finally the prophet *set his face to the Desert*
and *lifted his eyes*

and sees Israel
and does not curse,
and blesses the people outright.

3.

Who is to say your vantage point is God's?
Learn to look through God's eyes.


*Numbers 22:41 – 24:1-10*

*Abe Mezrich*

# Pinchas

# Immortality

1.
Zelofhad has no sons.
When Zelofhad dies,
his daughters say:
*Why should the name of our father be diminished?*
Let us inherit
from his ancestral land.
*

God says:
Zelofhad's daughters have spoken well.
If a man has no sons,
let his daughter inherit his ancestral land.

With no daughters,
let his brothers,
his uncles,
his nearest kin inherit his ancestral land.

Let his name survive
through his wide family.

2.
God tells Moses he will die.
Moses asks God for a successor.
And though Aaron's son succeeds Aaron,
God chooses Joshua to finish Moses' work:
Joshua, who is not of Moses' family at all.
Joshua brings the people into the Land.

3.
Our lives have boundaries:
ourselves,
our small circle.
And so we are limited.

*Abe Mezrich*

Our lives are so limited
that death can end us.
*

This is the only way
to stop death,
to become endless:
to reach to the people beyond us,
for the people beyond us to reach to us,
to end the boundaries.


*With thanks Kathi for help in working through this idea. And
for extending the circle.*

Numbers 20:22-29, Chapter 27

# Statecraft

1.
The men turn to idolatrous prostitutes
and God calls upon Moses
to hold the leaders accountable
and Moses calls upon the judges to act.

But soon there is no need.
Pinchas,
the lone man,
rises up and strikes two sinners before the congregation
and curtails God's wrath.

God declares Pinchas will be the next High Priest
and we read of Israel's families
and where in the Land they will dwell.

2.
In this vision of the future of Israel
the heads of state do not lead.
We do,
holding each other to what is right,
guiding each other like family

for we are family.


*Numbers Chapter 25 - 26*

*Abe Mezrich*

## Imperfect

These are mentioned in the genealogy:

Datan and Aviram *strove...against the Lord.*
*And the earth...swallowed them.*

Er and Onan, the sons of Yehudah,
*died in the Land of Cana'an*
        for they were *wicked in the eyes of the Lord.*

Nadav and Avihu, the sons of Aaron, *brought a strange fire*
*before* God; they are smitten down.

Zelophchad, of the tribe of Menashe, *died of his own sin*
and left no sons.


There are those who are so imperfect
they disappear.

Even they are a part of us.


*Genesis 38:7, 10; Numbers 26:9-10, 19, 61; 27:3*

# Reaching Out

1.
On the first day of Sukkot,
the final holiday,
offer thirteen bulls:
  one more than the number of tribes of Israel.
On the second, twelve bulls.
On the third, eleven.
By the seventh day, offer seven bulls:
  the number of the days of Creation.

On the eighth, offer one.

2.
Expand beyond the limits but do not stay.
Come back to the wholeness, to the essence:
nothing less or more.


*Numbers 29:12-38*

*Abe Mezrich*

# *Matot*

# How We Forge Our Own Path

1.
Moses teaches
the Laws of vows
and the Laws of oaths
to the tribal chieftains.

He teaches in the name of God.
Moses speaks
of the role a husband may play
in the vows of his wife
and the role a father may play
in the vows of his daughter.


2.
Through a vow
a person creates his own Law,
sets his own path.

Moses says
in the name of God:

Let the path each person sets
be of the world of women with men
of parents with children
of fathers with daughters.

Let each person's own path
be a path of interconnectedness,
of people in families in tribes within a nation

under God.


*Numbers 30:2 - 17*

*Abe Mezrich*

# How Far Must we Go?

1.
The tribes of Gad and Reuven
*had cattle in extremely great numbers.*
And the East side of the Jordan River,
before you enter the Land,
is a good *place for cattle.*

The tribes of Gad and Reuven tell Moses:
*Do not pass us through the Jordan*
into the Land.
>     Let us settle here, on the East of the Jordan.
>     Let us be cattlemen here.

Moses says: if you *pass yourselves…through the Jordan*
>     and help your brother-tribes settle the Land
then you may come back here, to the East;
>     and settle here.

2.
Also:
Utensils become impure whey they touch a dead body.
To purify them,
*any thing which can withstand fire, you must pass through fire*
*and any thing which cannot withstand fire,*
*you must pass through water.*

3.
Not everything is meant to *pass through fire.*
Some things are meant to *pass through water.*

Not everyone is meant to *pass through the Jordan* and stay.
Some are meant to *pass through the Jordan,*
and then to go back.

There are many ways in the world.
There are many ways to fulfill life.


*Numbers 31:19,23; Chapter 32 and especially verse 29*

## You Are More Than Just You

If you stay here to tend your own flocks,
you will be like your fathers
who refused the Land.

Realize: Your life belongs to history.


*Numbers Chapter 32*

## Three Lessons of Moses Demanding the Two Tribes Help Fight for The Land He Has Been Shut Out of, Destined to Die in the Desert Alone

1/

*You have risen up*
*a culture of sinful men*
The young can toss away
what the old can only dream of

2/

*We will not settle across the Jordan*
*we have already arrived to our land*
The old cannot force
the young to live the dream

3/

*And Moses said:*
*But you must march before God into battle*
*and they said:*
*We will march before God into battle*

The young have no right
no right
to let the dream slip away.


*Numbers Chapter 32, very loosely translated*

*Abe Mezrich*

# Masei

## Exchange

Moses details every place God took us on the way to the
Land

& God defines the boundaries of the Land He will take us
to.

We find our journey through the world through God,
& it is through us He defines a home.

*Numbers 33:1-34:15*

# What Can Death Offer Us?

1.
The Fall of Man
brings death to the world
and the Couple moves
to the East of Eden.
*
Abraham's father
dies in Haran.
God calls upon Abraham
to journey to the Land.
*
*Egypt*
*was burying*
their firstborn
*whom HaShem had struck*
and Israel embarked
out, into the Desert.
*
God says:
When you come to the Land
establish cities
for a man to flee to
if he kills by mistake;
to take refuge there
from the avenging family.
*
Death sparks a journey.


2.
Through death we know
there is not enough time
to wait to begin.

\*

Through death we know
that life is so small,
life cannot contain
the journey inside of us.

We must journey out
beyond where we live
to let this journey take place.
\*

So death sparks a journey:
it guides us to life.


*Genesis Chapter 3, 11:26-12:6; Numbers 33:3-49, 35:9-13*

## Boundaries

Other nations carve out a country conquest by conquest
until they have a land.

But God has said:
This is your country & its boundaries,
go enter it.

Thus, it is a gift.

This sacred gift is:
Borders to not go past,
boundaries to fill.


*Numbers 34:1-15*

## Whose Journey?

At the end of the forty-year journey
God guides us through

the heads of the families of Menashe
uncover a hidden challenge
in the laws of inheritance and marriage

& the heads of the families of Menashe
take the case to Moses
& ask that it be remedied

& Moses takes the case to the Holy One
Who agrees with the heads of the families.

So now we are the guides.


*Numbers 36:1 - 10*

# On the Edge of the Land
## The Book of Devarim

Between the journey and the arrival is anticipation.
Moses will die. The people will continue on. There is not
much time. There is so much to say. Moses offers one last
speech that, he hopes, will say all that is needed to be said.
Come, let us listen.

*Abe Mezrich*

# Devarim

## Reversal

In the Torah's last book Moses retells the story
& God chants a song
of things to come.

Before,
Moses spoke God's words
& people wrote poems,
sung songs:
like the song of Israel at the Sea.

Now, Moses speaks for himself,
and God writes a poem.

Now we speak as each other.


*A comment on the book as a whole*

*Abe Mezrich*

# Strife in the Nation

1.
You are a people filled with *strife*, Moses says.

So make a system of judges
throughout the nation
to *judge…between a man and his brother.*

And the people do this,
and the people travel forward.

2.
*All* the people approach Moses
asking to send spies to the Land.

But when the spies bring back word
the people are very frightened

the people *sulked in their* own *tents*
saying *our brothers*
*have sent fear into our hearts.*

And that is how a whole generation
rejects the Holy Land
and how God rejects a whole generation.

3.
We can unite around our differences and travel forward
or we can pretend we are seamlessly one, and fail.


*Deuteronomy 1:11-19, 22-36*
*(The word "sulked" from the JPS translation)*

# Why Hearing is a Responsibility

1.
Moses retells
the story of the Spies:
That they spy out the Land
that they return to the people
that they say:
*HaShem has given us a good Land.*
*

And then the people's response:
*Our brothers have melted our hearts;*
the Land is full of giants,
it is full of dangerous people,
it is a place God sends us to
in *hatred.*
*

For this lack of faith,
the people wander the Desert
for forty years.

2.
The people say
*Our brothers have melted our hearts,*
our brothers have immobilized us with fear;
yet the spies have said just one thing:
that the Land is *good.*

3.
People will say good things
and people will say bad things
but we will hear
what we will hear.

*Abe Mezrich*

We decide
what that will be
what we will be.


*Deuteronomy 1:22-36*

## Limits

1.
When the people come near to the land of Moav,
God warns the people to not enter battle with Moav.
For *I will not give you of* that nation's land, God says.
*I have already given it to the children of Lot.*

This warning comes before God gives the Israelites
victory over the Kingdom of Sichon
and over the Kingdom of Bashan
and over the Seven Kingdoms of the land of Canaan.

Before great conquest,
God warns the people Israel to not conquer.

2.
Even before we take,
God demands that we ask: *What will God not let me take?*

We must know that there are limits.

*Deuteronomy 2:17-19*

*Abe Mezrich*

# VaEtchanan

# God-Fearing

1.
God tells Moses:
gather the people
that they hear my words
*that they learn to fear Me.*
*

Later, Moses tells the people:
remember you *saw no image* then;
you *only* heard a *voice.*

Had you seen a vision
you could come to make an idol;
you could come to look to the sun,
the moon,
you could come to worship them,
you could craft spiritualities
from what you see.

2.
In this,
Moses says:
Seeing means looking to the world
to construct your worldview
from your own perspective
even if your perspective is wrong.

But God gathers the people
to learn to *fear* Him.

3.
Of course *fear* and *sight*
*yirah* and *ri'eyah*
are nearly one word
spelled differently.

\*

In fear, you also look to the world.
But not to find your own view.
You look,
and see how you are wholly dependent
on something else,
someone else.
You see yourself in the world's eyes,
another's eyes.

4.
Revelation begins not in looking,
but in fear:

perhaps to teach us to see
through someone else's perspective
through God's perspective
through God's eyes alone.

*Deuteronomy 4:9-20*

## Love Story

Do not look up to the sky
to worship the sun, moon, stars.
Other nations do this,
but not you.

You worship He Who Has Taken you
from the iron crucible of Egypt
to bring you close.

Others worship the things they see,
the given facts of the world.

Your worship is a love story.


*Deuteronomy 4:9-20*

# Revelation

*the mountain burned in fire up to the heavens,*
*and HaShem spoke from within the fire*

Not a great light from Heaven
but fire from the Mountain below,
making Heaven bright.


*Deuteronomy 4:11-12*

## Mercy

Before Moses retells the giving of the Ten Commandments,
he dedicates cities of refuge:
cities where accidental murderers can run to
& hide from avenging families.

Before we have Law, we must have mercy.


*Deuteronomy 4:41-5:18*


*Abe Mezrich*

# Eikev

## The Difference Between Weakness and Strength

1.
Moses recounts:
How God shepherded Israel in the Desert,
the frightening wasteland,
and how Israel will conquer the Land with God's help.

2.
The God who shepherds us in weakness
is the God who gives us strength.

To say: We are no more powerful when we are strong
than when we are weak.
And we are no more powerless when we are weak
than when we are strong.
Either way, we can do nothing without God's help.

3.
So that the difference between weakness and strength
does not exist.
And the difference between the strong and the weak
does not exist.

Only God's help exists.


*Deuteronomy 8:11 – 9:5*

*Abe Mezrich*

# Then and Now

*Remember the Sabbath day...for in six days HaShem made the Heavens and Earth, the Sea, and all that is in them; and on the seventh day, He rested.*

*Beware lest your forget HaShem* Who gave you manna: bread *which your fathers did not know.*

\*

Remember what God did at the beginning of time.
Do not forget that your own generation has witnessed God.

Remember that God has always been with the world.
Do not forget that God is in the world this very moment, in your very life.

*Exodus 8:20-11; Deuteronomy 8:14-16*
*(based on JPS translation)*

# Covenant

1.
At the Revelation there was smoke
and fire lighting the Heavens
and stone carved by God's own hand.

2.
Decades later Moses tells the people:
Your children will live in the Land for generations
but the covenant begins with you—
you, who have seen God's wonders
in Egypt that God took you from
and in the Desert God took you through.

3.
Where does the covenant begin?
Not with the sudden gift from the mountaintop
but in walking with God through lands, through years.

*Deuteronomy 4:9–13, 11:2-7*

# Tefillin

Remember: it is God
Who sends rain down from heaven
to the ground where we work.

Take this truth,
place it on your head
& on your arm.

Tie your strength below
to what is above.


*Deuteronomy 11:13-18*

*Abe Mezrich*

# Re'eh

## The Two Mountains

1.
At Mount Sinai we received what is good.

But we had no mountain for our wickedness
no place to take hold of it
and own it and shape it.

So we made it, instead,
into the Golden Calf,
there at the base of that same mountain.

2.
Entering the Land we announce blessing and curse:
blessing from the top of Mount Gerizim,
curse from the top of Mount Eival:
> Accursed is he who sets an idol in secret
> Accursed is he who moves his neighbor's boundary
> Accursed is he who sets a stumbling-block
> before the blind.

3.
A mountain for good,
a mountain for facing what is not good.

A people of God needs both.


*Exodus 19 and following; Exodus 32;*
*Deuteronomy 11:26-29, 27:11-26*

*Abe Mezrich*

# Specify

When you come to the land,
do not be like those who worship *upon the high mountains*
*and on the hills, and under every leafy tree.*
Worship at *the place that God will choose.*

*

Is your task to join the universe?
Or is it to fill up your one place,
—your tiny world?

*Deuteronomy 12:2-7*

*Based on the philosophy of Rav Ezra Bick*

# What You Own

Eat of an animal but not its blood
Gather your crop but leave over a tenth
Shear & work your flocks
       but not their firstborn
Own land
own people
be owed money
      but give it all up in six years
           (and leave your slave with a gift).

Own what you own
but you do not own the core of things.

The core is for the things themselves
and for God.
You are neither.


*Deuteronomy 12:15-16, 20-25; 14:22-15:15*

*Abe Mezrich*

# Land Law People

1.
In Leviticus,
       the book of offerings and purity
God tells Moses
on the mountaintop
at Sinai
in the Desert:

Every seven years
when you come to the Land
give the Land its Sabbath,
give the Land rest,
let the fields lie fallow.
Know that the Land is God's,
so nothing is yours.

2.
In Deuteronomy,
       the book at the edge of the Land
Moses speaks of the Sabbatical year also.

There, he does not speak
of fallow land.
He only says:
Every seven years
forgive each other's debts.

3.
When the Land is far away
a notion from the mountaintop
amidst mystical notions
we speak of kindness to God's Land.
When we go to settle it
we speak of kindness

to the Land's people.

4.
Come close to the Land,
and God's Land
becomes the people of God's Land.

Come close, and you cannot distinguish
God's mystical world
and the actual people you find there.


*Leviticus Chapter 25; Deuteronomy 15:1-11*
*Although: Note how the themes are intertwined in Exodus 23:10-11.*

*Inspired by Rabbi Menachem Leibtag*

*Abe Mezrich*

# Shoftim

# The Promised Land

1.
Moses says:
Let a judge not take bribes: for a bribe blinds justice.
Let a king not grow arrogant over his brothers.
Put down the false prophet.
Let the weak-hearted soldier go home
and not dishearten his comrades.
If you find a murdered corpse between cities
and cannot find the murderer,
let the city elders
from the closest city
hold a ceremony, to say:
we *did not shed this blood.*
*And you shall take away bloodshed,*
doing *what is right in God's eyes.*

2.
These are Laws
for a time of judges,
kings,
prophets,
wars,
elders:
an established life
in the Land of God's promise,
the Land with *the eyes of God upon it.*

These are Laws of bribe-taking judges
and arrogant kings
and false prophets
and cowardly soldiers
and city elders stumped by murder
near their own cities.

*Abe Mezrich*

That is the Promised Land.
It is like everywhere else.

3.

But here is the Promise:
a life with *the eyes of God upon it*;
and you doing *what is right in God's eyes*,
under God's eyes.

The Promise of an ordinary life,
with God.


*Deuteronomy 16:19, 17:14-20, 18:20, 20:1-9, 21:1-9*

# Ideal

1.
Your king may not amass horses,
lest he send you back to Egypt
the land of horses.

Do not take a king
from another nation.
Choose him *from amongst your brothers.*

2.
The tribe of Levi,
the tribe of the priests,
will have no tribal home.
Levi will be dispersed
across the people.

If a Levite wants,
he may journey to God's Temple
and serve there beside his *brothers.*

3.
Do not practice the pagan arts,
passing your children through fire;
turning to mediums to consult the dead.

Turn, instead, to the prophet
whom God has chosen
from amongst your *brothers.*

4.
Not the foreign, the majestic, the mystical—

but your brother:
here beside you.

*Deuteronomy 17:14-20 – 18:15*

*Abe Mezrich*

# Who is Moses?

1.
We were frightened
when God appeared to us at Sinai.

We told Moses then:
we will not survive this,
we cannot listen,
you listen for us.

God told Moses:
The people speak well.
You listen for them
and tell them what I will say.

After you, a new prophet will listen for them.
A prophet who, like you, is from among the people.
A prophet who, like you, will tell them what I will say.

2.
Moses is one through whom we remember
that God belongs to all of us
that God does not belong to any one of us
that we heard God together
that we were too small to stand before God
and that we have no personal spirit guides
and no private magicians.

We have Moses.
We have the prophets who follow after Moses,
prophets who are from among us.

3.
We hear God through our smallness.
We hear God through each other.

*Deuteronomy 18:9-22*

# Enemy

Do not fear the enemy in War. God is with you.

\*

If you have just built your house, do not come to battle
      lest you die and another will take it.
If you have just planted a vineyard, do not come to battle
      lest you die and another man will eat of it.
If you have just engaged a woman, do not come to battle
      lest you die and another man will marry her.
If you are frightened, do not come to battle
      lest you frighten those who are with you.

\*

With no enemy to fear, whom do we have to fear?
We have each other to fear.

Turn back, so this will not be so.
\*
God protects us from the world.
He leaves it to us
      to protect ourselves from us.

*Deuteronomy 20:1-10*

# Ki Teitze

# The Borders

In the Desert we learn
when to enter God's house
& when not to
when to enter the impure man's house
& when not to
we learn to respect
the boundaries of the spirit.

At the border of the Land
Moses tells us:
Bring your brother's lost animal
into your house
build a fence around your roof
so as to not bring blood into that house
stand outside the house
of the debtor whose collateral you collect.

In the Desert we learn
to revere the boundaries of the spirit.
In our new Land,
we are ready for the boundaries of each other.

Sacredness readies us for kindness.


*Leviticus 1 – 17; Deuteronomy 22:1-3,5; 24:11-13*

*Abe Mezrich*

# Pinnacles

The people of Babel
build a tower to reach the heavens,
a literal skyscraper.

But Moses says:
When you build a house,
place a fence around the roof
so those who climb to the top
will not fall.

A different kind of pinnacle:
not the great height,
but the safety we offer each other.


*Genesis 11:1-9; Deuteronomy 22:8*

# Why We Need Love in Wartime

1.
God said
*it is not good*
*for Man to be alone*
so He formed the Woman
for the man to come to,
to be with *as one flesh.*

*Therefore a man will leave his father*
*and his mother*
*and cling to his wife:*
therefore a man
will look beyond the family
beyond his group
and seek out this woman
this other
so that he will achieve this *good,*
so he will become fully human.

Thus God creates humanity.

2.
War is different.

In war,
we destroy the other
who is beyond us.

We achieve the opposite
of seeking out the other,
the opposite of
of *good,*
the opposite
of humanity.

*Abe Mezrich*

3.
A man in his first year of marriage
does not go to war.
He stays home
away from the battlefield,
from his countrymen,
*and he will make his wife happy.*

So even as we fight
we never can fully forsake
the ideal of engaging the other:
we never fully forsake
what is *good,*
we never fully forsake
what makes us human.

*Genesis 2:18, 21-25; Deuteronomy 23:5*

# Who is Someone's

Recognize your firstborn son
of your hated wife
as your firstborn son

send the bird away if you take her eggs
and she will not see her own loss

return your brother's lost sheep

bury the hanged man
take him down from the tree
and give him his final rest
(even he is made in God's image)

if you capture a war-bride
give her a month to sit in your home
and cry for her father and mother
listen to her cry
perhaps you will set her free

perhaps you will look at the people & animals of this world
& know that everyone is someone's child
& everyone belongs to God.


*Deuteronomy 21:10-22:7*

*Abe Mezrich*

# Ki Tavo

# Joy is a Duty

1.
Moses says:
*The Land you have arrived to*
*is not like the Land of Egypt*
*that grows seed* from abundant water
*like a garden of greens.*
The Land you have come to
is a Land of rain
but the rain does not always come.

2.
Moses says:
When you come to the Land
and your crop bears fruit
you must bring the first fruit
before God.
You must recite the history:
of the earliest days,
of slavery in Egypt,
of leaving Egypt,
of the Desert,
of arriving to the Land.
*You must rejoice in all the good*
*that HaShem has given you.*

3.
You come all the way from Egypt.
Rain comes all the way from the sky.
No one here is a native.
Everyone is an unexpected guest.
*

An unexpected guest, you have no reason to assume
a steady life with crops,
a watered garden.

\*

So all good is a surprise here.
And surprised, you come to joy.

4.
This joy
—this wonder at God's gifts—
is what you must announce.

This joy is your duty.

*Deuteronomy 11:10-12; 26:1-11*

*Possibly inspired by Micah Goodman's reading of this passage (I cannot remember if I thought of this idea before or after I encountered his).*

# Cycle

Pronounce
that you have given to God
of the fruits with which He has blessed you.

Pronounce
that you have given of your fruits
to the landless priest,
to the stranger & the orphan & the widow.

Pronounce
to God: look down from above
& bless us below.

*

If you know
that your fruits are from God,
you will share them.

If you share God's gifts,
you may ask for God's gifts.


*Deuteronomy 26:1-15*

# When You are Hidden from Others

1.
When you grow a crop, bring the first fruits before God.
*Respond* before the priest
      with the long story of God's kindness
      from the days of the fathers until now.

When you finish tithing, say to God:
*I have removed* the tithes *from my house,*
I have given my tithes away;
now You, God, *bless Your people Israel.*
      Now You, God, respond.

When you enter the Land, the whole nation
      must stand upon two mountains.
The Levites will *respond* with curse
      upon *whomever does evil in secret.*
*And the entire nation will respond:*
      Amen.

2.
When you speak of the fruit of your open field,
      you *respond.*
When you speak of the tithes hidden in your *house,*
      you ask God: Please respond.
When we speak of dark secrets,
      we *respond* to each other.

3.
We respond
      about what is open for all to see.
We ask for response
      about what others cannot see.
We respond to each other
      about what we would dare not show.

As we would withdraw into our own worlds,
we must reach beyond our separate world:
we must respond.


*Deuteronomy 26:1-15, Chapter 27*

# Beginnings

The covenant at Sinai.

Four decades later,
the covenant at the edge of the Land
*aside from the covenant* at Sinai.

What is the great revelation?
It is the start of the revelation to come.


*Deuteronomy 28:69*

*Abe Mezrich*

# Nitzavim

# Forever

1.
Each of you
—chieftains, elders, officers,
women, children
woodcutters,
water-bearers—
are entered into God's covenant.
Those who are here today,
those who are not yet here.

2.
In God's covenant we unite
        chieftains and woodcutters
        elders and children
        officers and water bearers
        the high and the low.
In God's covenant we are all together.

In God's covenant we unite
        those who are here
        with those who are not yet,
and time stretches back long ago
and forever ahead.

3.
It is in our togetherness
that our eternity comes.

*Deuteronomy 29:9-14*

*Abe Mezrich*

# Who You Are, Who You Must Be

1.
*You know how we dwelt in the land of Egypt*
*and that we passed through the midst of other nations*
*and you have seen the detestable things and the fetishes*
*of wood and stone,*
*silver and gold*

perhaps you will remember them and say:
*I follow my own willful heart*

\*

Your past can poison you
with passion to go back.
You are made from that past;
do not trust yourself.

Moses tells us so
on the cusp of entering the Land,
one moment before our future.

2.
Do not be what you were.
Do not be what you are.
Be who you must become.

*Deuteronomy 29:15-28*
*(JPS translation)*

## The Role of the Jews

Do right & the world will stand in awe of the nation to whom God has given wisdom. Do wrong & the world will know your downfall has come of your own sin. Either way you guide the nations to consider the ways of light. Your only choice is how you make the world see.

*Deuteronomy 4:6, 29:23-28*

# How a Book Holds us Responsible

1.
Moses says:
follow God's Laws
*that are written in this book.*

Moses says:
what I have commanded you
*is not in the sky*
that someone must go up
to bring it down;
*it is not across the sea*
that someone must cross the sea
to bring it to you.

*It is very close;*
it is *in your mouth*
*and in your heart*
*to do it.*

2.
God has handed His Book to Moses.
Moses has handed it to us.

Anyone can read this book.
Anyone can render it
the words on his lips,
anyone can carry it
to the depths of his heart.

3.
This takes away the excuse
of those who do not do—
who say:
I am waiting for the great man

to appear from far away
to give me guidance.

The great man has come
God has given him the book
to give to you.

Now, the book is in your hands.


*Deuteronomy 30:11-14*

*Abe Mezrich*

# VaYeilech

# Why We Sing

1.
The people see God's *great hand* at the Sea
*and believe* in God who has saved them from Egypt
and sing a song of praise.

When you see God's hand in your world,
in your life,
you sing.

2.
In the Land
God will give the people houses they did not build
wells they did not dig
vineyards and olive groves
they did not plant

and the people will grow satisfied in all this
and forget God in all this
though God has given them everything.

So before they arrive,
God gives them a song
to warn them not to forget.

3.
We sing because we see God before our eyes,
and we sing to remember to see.

*Exodus 14:30 – 15:19; Deuteronomy 6:10-12, 31:16-21*

# Passing the Words

1.
The king reads the Teaching,
and the whole people
—men, women, children—
gather to hear the king read the Teaching.

The king reads the words
and a nation springs up about him.

\*

In the beginning,
God said *Let there be light*
and finally *let there be humankind*
and a universe sprang up about Him.
Like the people, now,
listening,
spring up about the king.

2.
God has given us the words
and it is now our job to create with those words,
to be created with them.


*Genesis Chapter 1, Deuteronomy 31:10-13*

## Of the Book

1.
God tells Moses:
there will be times
when the people will stray from Me
and I, too, then,
will turn from the people.

Write this truth down,
a *testimony*
to the people for all time.

And Moses writes this warning into a book.

2.
So that when the people do not turn to God
and God does not turn to the people
this writing,
this book
still speaks between them.

3.
Through this book, perhaps,
we will find our way back to each other.


*Deuteronomy 31:15-30*

*Abe Mezrich*

# The Elect

1.
God tells Moses: the people will ultimately desert Me.
It is their nature.
And trouble will come upon them.

God tells Moses: before the people enter the Land,
write this truth down for them for time to come.
Let them know.

2.
Which Moses does.
And he tells the people: Guard this warning close
—*it is your life*.
It will keep you long on the Land.

3.
If you have been invited into God's kingdom,
you might think:
I am one of the elect; I can do no wrong.
You might think you are flawless.
You will fail to see your own nature.

This leaves you in danger from yourself.

4.
So:
Before you enter the Land of God,
what is the first thing you must do?
First you must face who you are.

*Deuteronomy 31:16 – 32:47*

*Abe Mezrich*

# Ha'azinu

# Hold the World Together

**1.**
The people of Babel fear they will scatter across the world.
They build a great tower from the valley where they live,
up to Heaven.
This, they think, will hold them in place;
will hold them together.

But God disbands them.


Far later God relays a speech for Moses to share.
In it, God calls Heaven and Earth to witness His words—
*like storms upon the vegetation.*
To remain a people on the Land, God says, follow God.

**2.**
In Babel they thought earth and sky and each of us
are separate things.
It would take a structure to connect them
for us to stay together.
But God tells Moses: Heaven and Earth and the people
and our lives with God
—they are already part of one fabric:
> a single fabric beneath the One God
> Who rains from the sky to the grass.

**3.**
If you want to the hold the world together,
do not invent a new structure to hold it up.
There is no need. It will not work.

Look to the fabric of God.
Fasten yourself to it.

*Genesis Chapter 11; Deuteronomy 31:16 - 32:2,44-47*

# Becoming

1.
God creates the *Heavens and the Earth*
and sees the *desolation* of the universe
and looks into infinite darkness
and utters: *Let there be light.*

2.
Before Moses dies
God gives him a poem
to share with the people.

The poem calls *Heaven and Earth* to bear witness.
The poem speaks
of how God took Israel from a *desolate* land
and of God's battle against wickedness throughout time.

3.
In the poem,
a desolate universe
becomes a desolate land we walk upon;
the Heaven and Earth that hear God speak
against the Cosmic Darkness
become the Heaven and Earth that hear God's words
against the darkness people make.

4.
God responds to the cosmic darkness
and the Torah begins.

By the end of the story,
we are the cosmos.

*Genesis Chapter 1, Deuteronomy Chapter 32*

## Place of Questions

Moses' parting song is this:
Be righteous enough for God to keep you in the Land.

Moses shares these words as a warning.
Because our righteousness is in question.


Then Moses dies where he is.
God never lets him into the Land.


Moses, more righteous than any of us, may not enter.
Only we whose righteousness is in question may enter.

Perhaps the Land is not there for the righteous.
It is there for the question.



*Deuteronomy Chapter 32*

———

*Based on Christine Hayes' reading of Jacob; and in memory of Robert Stone*

*Abe Mezrich*

# Book of Ruth

## Moab

The Moabites refused us *bread & water* in the Desert
& so now they may not marry us.

Moses failed to sanctify God
—he shouted at the thirsty people
as he took water from the rock—
& so he may not enter the Land;
he dies in Moab.

Moab is food & water never given
a kind word left unsaid
love that cannot happen
a traveler locked in the desert
longing for his Land.

## Ruth the Moabite

Ruth the Moabite
loves Naomi like a mother
follows Naomi in her love
leaves her people, her life in Moab
journeys with Naomi to the Land
all the way to *Beth Lehem*: *The House of Bread*
and she *does kindness* for Naomi there
and she marries Boaz, Naomi's kinsman, there.

Ruth is the bread, the water, the love, the journey,
shared at last
freed from Moab at last
arrived in the Land at last.

**Kingdom of David**
David,
king of Israel,
is the great-grandson of Ruth.

What family will reign in Israel?
One that unleashes the good trapped within.

*Numbers 20:1-13; Deuteronomy 23:4-5, 32:48-52; The Book of Ruth*

*Abe Mezrich*

# V'zot Habracha

# Covering

1.
Cain murders Abel
in a fit of jealousy.
Who buries him?
We do not know.
Perhaps no one buries him.
*Your brother's blood cries up from the ground*
God tells Cain.
Perhaps the blood is uncovered:
that is why its cry rises up.

2.
The other rival brothers
>   Isaac/Ismael
>   Jacob/Esau
>   Joseph/the other eleven
set aside their struggle
to bury their fathers together.

They bury the cry
(at least for a time).

3.
All of this is to say:
Burial buries the anger away.
Burial buries the cry
& makes peace possible up on the ground.

4.
At the end of the Five Books of our struggles with God
>   struggles in the Garden
>   struggles in the Flood
>   through the Calf
>   in the Desert

—in the end, God gives Moses a burial
there in the valley:

Moses, the best of all humanity
who has himself done wrong
who dies in his sin
who proves that none of us will not fail God.

God Himself gives Moses his burial.

5.
The history shows we will always struggle with God.
The conclusion shows that even so God will show us peace.


*Genesis 4:1-10, 25:9, 35:29, 50:12-14; Deuteronomy 34:6*

# The Holy Life

1.
God says to Moses:
Come up,
see the Land from afar,
from up on this mountain.
Then you will die.

For you will not enter the Land
because you did not sanctify Me
at the Waters of Strife.

Joshua
your disciple you lay hands upon
will bring your holiness to the people
will march down below among the people
will take the people to the Land.


2.
To be Moses on a mountain with God
is the peak of holiness.

To be Moses on a mountain with God
is also a punishment:
held on the mountain
kept from the Land
kept from the people
who will enter the Land.


3.
Here at the close of the Torah,
it is Joshua's form of holiness
we and Moses pine for.

Here at the close of the Torah,
we do not want to be on the mountain.
We want to be in the Land.


*Deuteronomy 34*

# Where is Torah?

Moses dies on the mountain with God
and God buries Moses in the valley.

It is like when God gave us Law.
God came down from above
and joined Moses on the mountain
and Moses went down from the mountain
and joined the people below the mountain.
Only then did God give us Law.

Now at the end of the book
we have received the whole Law;
now we must take it with us;
and God and Moses come from the sky,
the mountain,
the level ground,
down into the valley.

So at the end of the book,
a secret:
Even very low down
even in the valley
you are at the level of Moses and God.
Even in the valley
you are at the Torah's level.

*Exodus 19:20-20:14; Deuteronomy 34*

*Abe Mezrich*

## After

Moses sees the Land from afar,
the Land we will live in without him.

How will we live in the Land without Moses?

But it is not Moses' question to answer.

As the book we have just finished,
—Moses' book—
is not his book to live.

Now we must answer the question.
And the book is us.

*Deuteronomy 34*

*Abe Mezrich*

# About Abe Mezrich

Abe Mezrich uses contemporary poetry and prose to explore Jewish sacred themes, and sacred Jewish texts to understand our place in the world. His writing (including versions of some of the poems in this book) has appeared in *929, Hevriah, The Forward, The Los Angeles Jewish Journal, Lehrhaus, The New York Jewish Week,* and *Zeek.* His first book, *The House at the Center of the World: Poetic Midrash on Sacred Space,* is also available through Ben Yehuda Press. He lives with his wife Kathi and their three children. Learn more at www.abemezrich.com.

# The Jewish Poetry Project

## *Ben Yehuda Press*

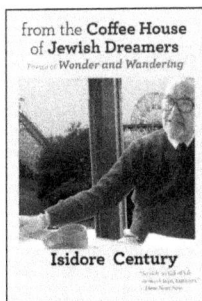

**From the Coffee House of Jewish Dreamers: Poems of Wonder and Wandering and the Weekly Torah Portion by Isidore Century**

"Isidore Century is a wonderful poet. His poems are funny, deeply observed, without pretension." – *The Jewish Week*

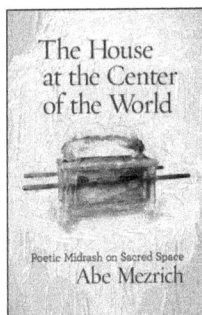

**The House at the Center of the World: Poetic Midrash on Sacred Space by Abe Mezrich**

"Direct and accessible, Mezrich's midrashic poems often tease profound meaning out of his chosen Torah texts. These poems remind us that our Creator is forgiving, that the spiritual and physical can inform one another, and that the supernatural can be carried into the everyday."
—Yehoshua November, author of *God's Optimism*

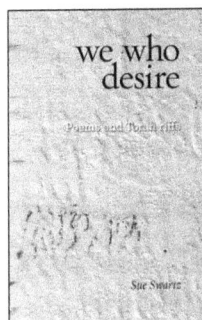

**we who desire: Poems and Torah riffs by Sue Swartz**

"Sue Swartz does magnificent acrobatics with the Torah. She takes the English that's become staid and boring, and adds something that's new and strange and exciting. These are poems that leave a taste in your mouth, and you walk away from them thinking, what did I just read? Oh, yeah. It's the Bible."
—Matthue Roth, author, *Yom Kippur A Go-Go*

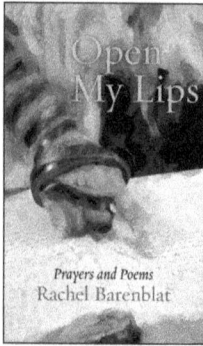

## Open My Lips: Prayers and Poems
## by Rachel Barenblat

"Barenblat's God is a personal God—one who lets her cry on His shoulder, and who rocks her like a colicky baby. These poems bridge the gap between the ineffable and the human. This collection will bring comfort to those with a religion of their own, as well as those seeking a relationship with some kind of higher power."
—Satya Robyn, author, *The Most Beautiful Thing*

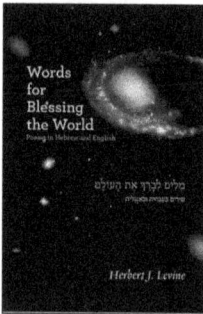

## Words for Blessing the World: Poems in
## Hebrew and English by Herbert J. Levine

"These writings express a profoundly earth-based theology in a language that is clear and comprehensible. These are works to study and learn from."
—Rodger Kamenetz, author, *The Jew in the Lotus*

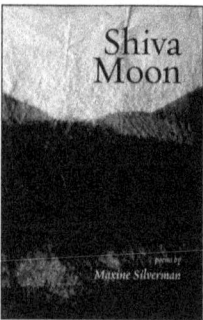

## Shiva Moon: Poems by Maxine Silverman

"The poems, deeply felt, are spare, spoken in a quiet but compelling voice, as if we were listening in to her inner life. This book is a precious record of the transformation saying Kaddish can bring. It deserves to be read. These are works to study and learn from."
—Howard Schwartz, author, *The Library of Dreams*

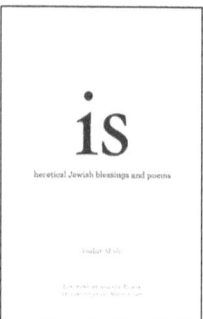

## is: heretical Jewish blessings and poems
## by Yaakov Moshe (Jay Michaelson)

"Finally, Torah that speaks to and through the lives we are actually living: expanding the tent of holiness to embrace what has been cast out, elevating what has been kept down, advancing what has been held back, reveling in questions, revealing contradictions."
—Eden Pearlstein, aka eprhyme

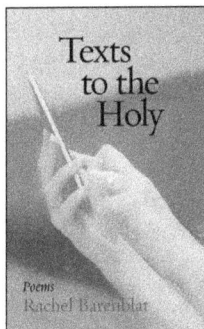

## Texts to the Holy: Poems
### by Rachel Barenblat

"These poems are remarkable, radiating a love of God that is full bodied, innocent, raw, pulsating, hot, drunk. I can hardly fathom their faith but am grateful for the vistas they open. I will sit with them, and invite you to do the same."
—Merle Feld, author of A Spiritual Life.

## The Sabbath Bee: Love Songs to Shabbat
### by Wilhelmina Gottschalk

"Torah, say our sages, has seventy faces. As these prose poems reveal, so too does Shabbat. Here we meet Shabbat as familiar housemate, as the child whose presence transforms a family, as a spreading tree, as an annoying friend who insists on being celebrated, as a woman, as a man, as a bee, as the ocean."
—Rachel Barenblat, author, The Velveteen Rabbi's Haggadah

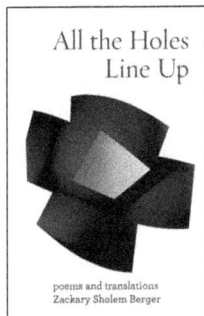

## All the Holes Line Up: Poems and Translations
### by Zackary Sholem Berger

"Spare and precise, Berger's poems gaze unflinchingly at—but also celebrate—human imperfection in its many forms. And what a delight that Berger also includes in this collection a handful of his resonant translations of some of the great Yiddish poets." —Yehoshua November, author of God's Optimism and Two World Exist

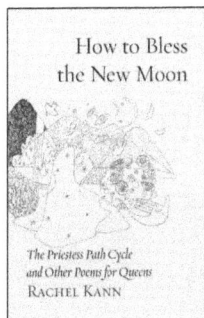

## How to Bless the New Moon: The Priestess Paths Cycle and Other Poems for Queens
### by Rachel Kann

"To read Rachel Kann's poems is to be confronted with the possibility that you, too, are prophet and beloved, touched by forces far beyond your mundane knowing. So, dear reader, enter into the 'perfumed forcefield' of these words—they are healing and transformative."
—Rabbi Jill Hammer, co-author of The Hebrew Priestess

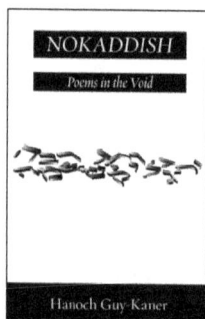

www.ingramcontent.com/pod-product-compliance
Lightning Source LLC
LaVergne TN
LVHW041338080426
835512LV00006B/515